The Legislative Branch

By Tracy Vonder Brink

Table of Contents

THE LEGISLATIVE BRANCH. 3
WORDS TO KNOW 22
INDEX 23
COMPREHENSION QUESTIONS 23
ABOUT THE AUTHOR. 24

A Starfish Book

SEAHORSE PUBLISHING

Teaching Tips for Caregivers:

As a caregiver, you can help your child succeed in school by giving them a strong foundation in language and literacy skills and a desire to learn to read.

This book helps children grow by letting them practice reading skills.

Reading for pleasure and interest will help your child to develop reading skills and will give your child the opportunity to practice these skills in meaningful ways.

- Encourage your child to read on her own at home
- Encourage your child to practice reading aloud
- Encourage activities that require reading
- Establish a reading time
- Talk with your child
- Give your child writing materials

Teaching Tips for Teachers:

Research shows that one of the best ways for students to learn a new topic is to read about it.

Before Reading

- Read the "Words to Know" and discuss the meaning of each word.
- Read the back cover to see what the book is about.

During Reading

- When a student gets to a word that is unknown, ask them to look at the rest of the sentence to find clues to help with the meaning of the unknown word.
- Ask the student to write down any pages of the book that was confusing to them.

After Reading

- Discuss the main idea of the book.
- Ask students to give one detail that they learned in the book by showing a text dependent answer from the book.

The Legislative Branch

The U.S. government has three **branches**.

The legislative branch makes **national** laws.

Congress runs the legislative branch.

It meets in the U.S. Capitol Building in Washington, D.C.

The people who serve in Congress are **elected** by each state.

Congress has two parts.

The House of Representatives is one part. It has 435 voting members.

States with more people elect more representatives.

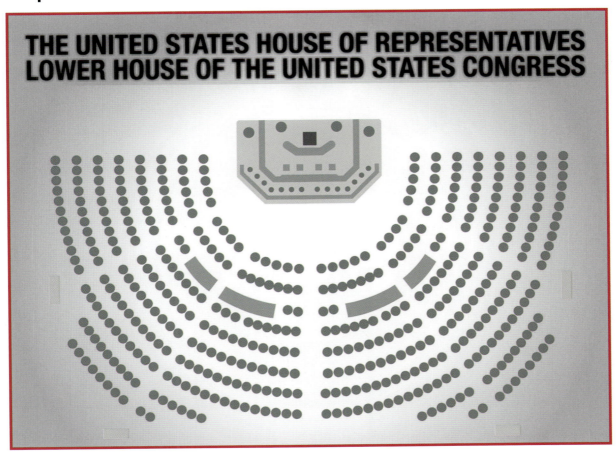

Members of the House serve for two years.

The Senate is the other part of Congress.

Each state elects two senators.

The Senate has 100 members.

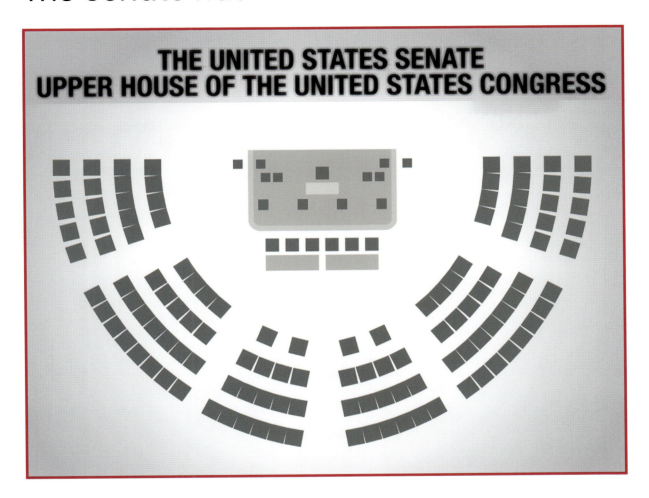

Members of the Senate serve for six years.

Congress works together to make new laws.

A law is an important rule that everyone must follow.

A bill is an idea for a new law.

A bill may start in the House or the Senate.

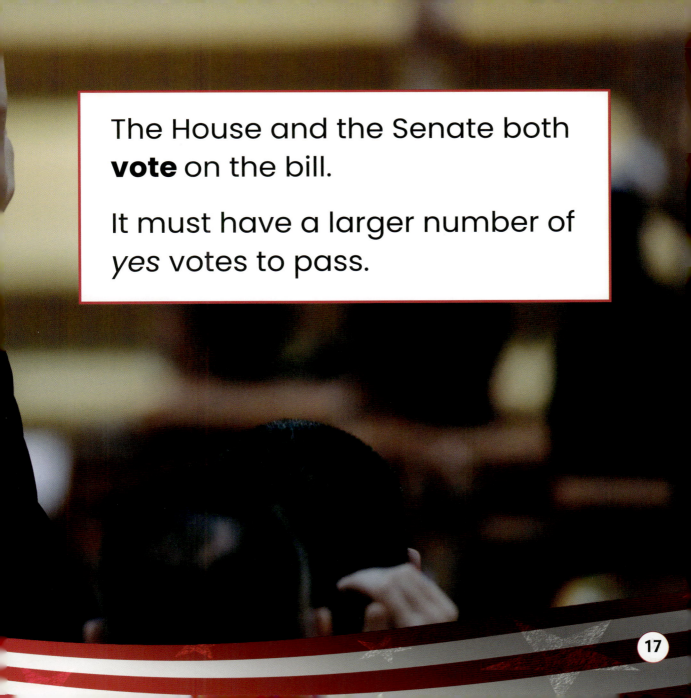

The House and the Senate both **vote** on the bill.

It must have a larger number of *yes* votes to pass.

A bill that passes goes to the **president**.

It becomes a law if the president approves it.

But the president may say no.

When a president says no to a bill, it's called a veto.

Congress may vote again.

But almost all must say yes to pass it.

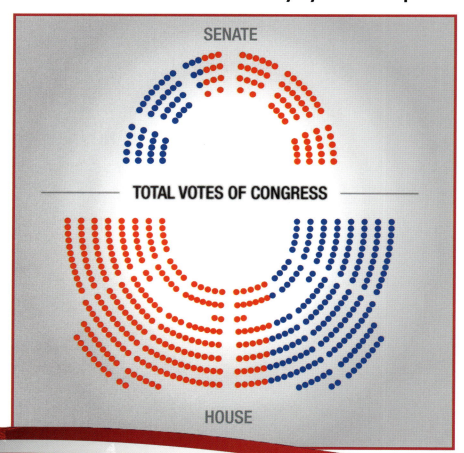

New laws take a lot of work.

Words to Know

branches (BRANCH-es): main parts of a government

Congress (CON-gruhs): the group of people in the U.S. government who make laws

elected (uh-LEKT-uhd): chose by voting

national (NASH-uh-nuhl): of or having to do with an entire country or nation

president (PREZ-uh-dent): the head of the government in some countries, such as the United States

vote (voht): to make a choice for or against someone or something

Index

bill 14, 15, 17, 18
Congress 4, 6, 10, 12, 20
House 8, 9, 15, 17
law(s) 3, 12, 14, 18, 21
president 18
Senate 10, 11, 15, 17

Comprehension Questions

1. What is a bill?
   a. something your parents pay each month
   b. an idea for a new law
   c. a part of an animal
2. There are _____ U.S. branches of government.
   a. three   b. two   c. one
3. After Congress votes yes, who needs to approve a bill for it to become a new law?
   a. citizens   b. Congress   c. the president
4. **True or False:** Laws are rules everyone must follow.
5. **True or False:** Congress is made up of two parts, the Senate and the House of Representatives.

Answers: 1.b 2.a 3.c 4.True 5.True

About the Author

Tracy Vonder Brink enjoys learning about the United States. She has visited the U.S. Capitol Building in Washington, D.C. Tracy lives in Cincinnati with her husband, two daughters, and two rescue dogs.

Written by: Tracy Vonder Brink
Design by: Kathy Walsh
Editor: Kim Thompson

Library of Congress PCN Data
The Legislative Branch / Tracy Vonder Brink
Civic Readiness
ISBN 978-1-63897-085-9 (hard cover)
ISBN 978-1-63897-171-9 (paperback)
ISBN 978-1-63897-257-0 (EPUB)
ISBN 978-1-63897-343-0 (eBook)
Library of Congress Control Number: 2021945257

Printed in the United States of America.

Photographs/Shutterstock: Cover, Pg 1 © MDart10, ©Vertes Edmond Mihai: Pg 1, 4-21 ©Lightspring: Pg 3 ©lunamarina: Pg 4 ©Peter Hermes Furian: Pg 5 ©RozenskiP: Pg 6 ©Rob Crandall: Pg 8 ©DCStockPhotography: Pg 9, 11 ©Angel Soler Gollonet: Pg 10 ©danielo: Pg 13 ©Freedomz: Pg 14©fizkes, ©Natcha Rochana: Pg 16 © M.Moira: Pg 18 ©natatravel: Pg 19 ©mark reinstein: Pg 20 ©natatravel: Pg 21©G-Stock Studio

Seahorse Publishing Company
www.seahorsepub.com

Copyright © 2022 **SEAHORSE PUBLISHING COMPANY**

All rights reserved. No part of this publication may be reproduced, stored in a retrieval system or be transmitted in any form or by any means, electronic, mechanical, photocopying, recording, or otherwise, without the prior written permission of Seahorse Publishing Company.

Published in the United States
Seahorse Publishing
PO Box 771325
Coral Springs, FL 33077